United States Presidents

Martin Van Buren

Anne Welsbacher

ABDO Publishing Company

visit us at
www.abdopub.com

Published by ABDO Publishing Company 4940 Viking Drive, Edina, Minnesota 55435.
Copyright © 2001 by Abdo Consulting Group, Inc. International copyrights reserved in
all countries. No part of this book may be reproduced in any form without written
permission from the publisher.

Published 2001
Printed in the United States of America
Second Printing 2002

Photo credits: Corbis

Edited by Bob Italia, Tamara L. Britton, Kate A. Furlong, Christine Phillips

Library of Congress Cataloging-in-Publication Data

Welsbacher, Anne, 1955-
    Martin Van Buren / Anne Welsbacher.
        p. cm. -- (United States presidents)
    Includes index.
    Summary: Examines the life and career of the eighth American president, who
had the nickname "Old Kinderhook."
    ISBN 1-57765-238-X
    1. Van Buren, Martin, 1782-1862--Juvenile literature. 2. Presidents-United
States--Biography--Juvenile literature. [1. Van Buren, Martin, 1782-1862.
2. Presidents.] I. Title. II. Series: United States presidents (Edina, Minn.)
E387.W47 1999
973.5'7'092--dc21
  [B]   98-4338
                                         CIP
                                         AC

Contents

Martin Van Buren

*M*artin Van Buren was the eighth president of the United States. When he was young, he studied to be a **lawyer**. Then he started working in **politics**.

Van Buren served in many public offices. He was a state **senator**, a U.S. senator, and governor of New York. He also served as **secretary of state** and vice president. Then in 1836, Van Buren was elected president.

As president, Van Buren led America through the Panic of 1837. He solved problems between Canada, the U.S., and Great Britain. He also oversaw wars with Native Americans.

Van Buren kept working in politics after he left the White House. He ran for president two more times. Then he spent several years traveling through Europe. He died in 1862.

Van Buren was an important American leader. He is best remembered for founding America's first **political machine**, establishing an independent **treasury**, and fighting against the spread of slavery.

Martin Van Buren

Martin Van Buren (1782-1862)
Eighth President

BORN:	December 5, 1782
PLACE OF BIRTH:	Kinderhook, New York
ANCESTRY:	Dutch
FATHER:	Abraham Van Buren (1737-1817)
MOTHER:	Maria Hoes Van Alen Van Buren (1747-1817)
WIFE:	Hannah Hoes (1783-1819)
CHILDREN:	Four boys
EDUCATION:	Village schools; studied in law office
RELIGION:	Dutch Reformed
OCCUPATION:	Lawyer, senator
MILITARY SERVICE:	None
POLITICAL PARTY:	Democrat

OFFICES HELD:	Surrogate of Columbia County, New York; New York state senator; attorney general of New York; U.S. senator; governor of New York; secretary of state; vice president
AGE AT INAUGURATION:	54
YEARS SERVED:	1837-1841
VICE PRESIDENT:	Richard M. Johnson
DIED:	July 24, 1862, Kinderhook, New York, age 79
CAUSE OF DEATH:	Natural causes

Birthplace of Martin Van Buren

Young Martin

*M*artin Van Buren was born in Kinderhook, New York, on December 5, 1782. He was the first president born in the United States of America. All presidents before him had been born in the British colonies.

Martin's parents were Abraham and Maria Van Buren. They farmed the land and owned a tavern. The Van Buren family was large. Martin had three sisters and two brothers. He also had two half-brothers and one half-sister.

Martin went to a one-room schoolhouse in Kinderhook. But he could not go to school often. He had to work on the farm and in the tavern.

While working in the tavern, Martin met **lawyers**, businessmen, and **politicians**. He often listened to them talk. He learned about current events in the U.S. and around the world.

Though Martin had little early education, he became a lawyer at the age of 21.

Learning the Law

*I*n 1796, Van Buren became an **apprentice**. He worked with a **lawyer** named Francis Sylvester. Sylvester's family liked Van Buren. They taught him good manners. They taught him how to dress well, too.

The Sylvesters were active in **politics**. They belonged to the **Federalist** party. It favored a strong national government and laws to help the rich. The Sylvesters wanted Van Buren to be a Federalist.

Van Buren did not want to be a Federalist. He agreed with the **Republican** party. It favored a government that would help the common people, not just the rich.

Van Buren and the Sylvesters disagreed on politics. But Van Buren stayed on as an apprentice. In 1803, he passed the **bar exam**. This allowed him to work as a lawyer. He started a successful law firm in Kinderhook.

Van Buren soon became interested in local **politics**. He worked to protect small farmers from large landowners.

In 1807, he married his childhood sweetheart and distant cousin, Hannah Hoes. They had four sons, Abraham, John, Smith, and Martin, Jr.

Hanna Hoes Van Buren

Life as a Politician

*I*n 1808, Van Buren got his first job in **politics**. He served as **surrogate** of Columbia County. He worked with the county's landowners. This allowed him to meet many powerful New Yorkers.

In 1812, Van Buren won a seat in the New York **senate**. Senator Van Buren supported the **War of 1812**. He passed laws to help New York protect itself against the British.

The Erie Canal

Senator Van Buren also supported a bill to build the Erie Canal. It connected the Hudson River with the Great Lakes. This improved **transportation** in New York.

Senator Van Buren also led a group called the Bucktails. They were against DeWitt Clinton. Clinton was New York City's powerful mayor. The Bucktails believed he had been disloyal to the **Republican** party.

Van Buren became New York's **attorney general** in 1818. He worked to end **debtor's** prison. People went to debtor's prison if they had large debts. Van Buren felt it was unfair to jail people for being poor.

But Van Buren's old rival DeWitt Clinton was elected

DeWitt Clinton

governor in 1817. In 1819, Clinton removed Van Buren from his job as attorney general. That same year, Van Buren's wife died.

Van Buren's Machine

Van Buren and the Bucktails continued to fight Clinton. They did not want him to be governor any longer. But New Yorkers re-elected Clinton in 1820.

Clinton's re-election angered the Bucktails. They began passing laws to change New York's government. At the same time, Van Buren worked to create a new **political** system. He hoped it would **unite Republicans** and make the party more powerful.

In Van Buren's system, he made sure many Bucktails got government jobs. Some of them were not qualified. But because they were Bucktails, Van Buren gave them jobs anyway. This is called the **spoils system**.

Van Buren used the spoils system in a new way. He united **senators** from all over the state into a powerful group. It stopped Governor Clinton from passing laws.

Van Buren's group became America's first **political machine**. It was called the Albany Regency. The Albany Regency lasted for nearly fifty years.

Van Buren knew he had many supporters in the Albany Regency. So he decided to run for the U.S. **Senate**. He won the election of 1821. Soon, he was off to Washington, D.C.

New York City Hall

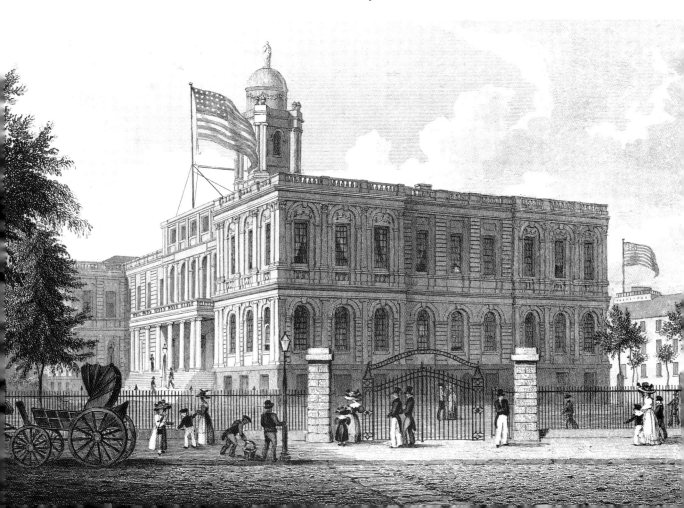

The Making of the Eighth United States President

1782 ➡ Born December 5 in Kinderhook, New York

1796 ➡ Becomes lawyer's apprentice

1803 ➡ Passes the bar, becomes a lawyer

1807 ➡ Marries Hannah Hoes

➡ **1818** ➡ Becomes New York state attorney general

1819 ➡ Wife Hannah dies; removed from attorney general position

1821 ➡ Elected to U.S. Senate

1829 ➡ Appointed secretary of state by President Jackson

1836 Elected president

1837 Panic of 1837; refuses to annex Texas

1838 Trail of Tears

1840 Passes independent treasury bill; Harrison elected president

1844 ➡ Runs for president but does not get the nomination

PRESIDENTIAL YEARS

Martin Van Buren

"From a small community we have risen to a people powerful in numbers and strength; but with our increase has gone hand in hand the progress of just principles."

1808
Serves as surrogate for Columbia County

1812
Elected to New York state senate; War of 1812

Historic Events during Van Buren's Presidency

Michigan admitted as a state

Abner Doubleday leads the first baseball game ever played

Kirkpatrick Macmillan builds the first bicycle

1832
Elected vice president under President Jackson

1835
Seminole War begins

1845
Leads Barnburners; Texas annexed to U.S.

1848
Runs for president but loses election

1852
Travels in Europe

1855
Returns to Kinderhook; writes *Autobiography*

1862
Dies on July 24

Van Buren in Washington

*V*an Buren was a U.S. **senator** for seven years. He headed two major **committees**. He did not speak often. But he could argue well and knew his facts.

Senator Van Buren favored a small federal government and states' rights. Other **politicians** agreed with Van Buren. So President Jackson, Senator Van Buren, and other politicians organized the **Democratic** party.

In 1828, Van Buren wrote a bill to make Florida a state. This angered some people because Florida had slavery. So he said people who already owned slaves could keep them. But no one could buy more slaves. This idea won Van Buren much respect.

Later in 1828, Van Buren became governor of New York. He improved banks and changed election laws. In 1829, President Andrew Jackson made him **secretary of state**.

As **secretary of state**, Van Buren continued to use the **spoils system**. He encouraged President Jackson to use it, too. Van Buren also led President Jackson's **advisors**, known as the **Kitchen Cabinet**. And he made **treaties** with other countries.

In 1832, the **Democrats** held their first **convention**. They chose Van Buren for vice president. He ran with President Jackson. They won the election.

Jackson and Van Buren fought against the Bank of the United States. They felt it was too powerful and only helped the rich. The bank closed in 1836.

President Andrew Jackson

Later that year, Jackson helped Van Buren run for president. Van Buren won the election.

President Van Buren

*S*hortly after Van Buren took office, the Panic of 1837 began. Banks ran out of money. People lost their jobs. Businesses failed.

To fix the problem, Van Buren asked **Congress** to form an independent **treasury**. It would be a bank just for government money. He thought it would prevent another **depression**.

Congress voted against Van Buren's treasury. They thought it would help the government but not the people.

During this time, Texas **declared** its independence from Mexico. It wanted to be **annexed** to the U.S.

But Van Buren worried that annexing Texas would start a war with Mexico. He also worried that if Texas became a state, it would have slavery. This would have angered many Americans. So Van Buren did not annex Texas.

Next Van Buren faced problems with Canada. The Canadians wanted independence from Great Britain. Some Americans **volunteered** to help. They sent a supply ship called the *Caroline*. British soldiers attacked the *Caroline* and killed many of the Americans on board.

The British attack upset Americans. So Van Buren sent troops to the Canadian border. But he told them not to fight. Then he helped Canada and Great Britain work out a **compromise**.

In 1838, the U.S. government forced the Cherokee Native Americans to leave their homelands. It wanted the land for white settlers. U.S. troops forced the Cherokee to walk to a **reservation** in present-day Oklahoma. Thousands of Cherokee died on the journey. It is known as the Trail of Tears.

U.S. troops also fought Seminole Native Americans for land in Florida. The Seminole War had started in 1835. The war was costly. Thousands of Americans and Seminole died.

The Cherokee walked 1,200 miles (1,931 km) on the Trail of Tears.

In 1839, Van Buren faced more problems with Canada. The U.S. and Canada disagreed about the border between Maine and New Brunswick, Canada. Both countries were ready for war.

Seminole in their Florida homeland

General Winfield Scott

President Van Buren sent General Winfield Scott to the area. Scott made an agreement between both sides. They decided to let a boundary commission decide who owned the land. The commission split the land between both countries.

In 1840, Van Buren changed his plan for an independent **treasury**. This time, **Congress** accepted it.

Also in 1840, Van Buren ran for re-election. Some of the events in Van Buren's presidency made him unpopular. He lost to William Henry Harrison. Van Buren left the White House and returned to Kinderhook.

The United States during Van Buren's presidency

Existing States

Existing Territories

Disputed Territory

The Seven "Hats" of the U.S. President

To be president, a person must have lived in the country for at least 14 years, must be a U.S. citizen born in America, and must be at least 35 years old.

A president is elected or re-elected every four years.

Chief of State
- Performs official duties
- Stands as a symbol of the United States

Chief Diplomat
- Oversees relations with other countries
- Writes treaties
- Grants recognition to new governments

Chief Executive
- Oversees government programs
- Manages government workers

Commander-in-Chief
- Constructs military plans
- Maintains control of armed forces

Chief Legislator
- Proposes laws
- Reports to Congress

Chief Politician
- Leads political party
- Supports its candidates

Chief Jurist
- Appoints federal judges
- Enforces court rulings

If a president dies in office, the vice president becomes president.

A president can serve only two terms. Each term lasts four years. When Van Buren was president, this law did not exist.

As president, Martin Van Buren had seven jobs.

The Three Branches
of the U.S. Government

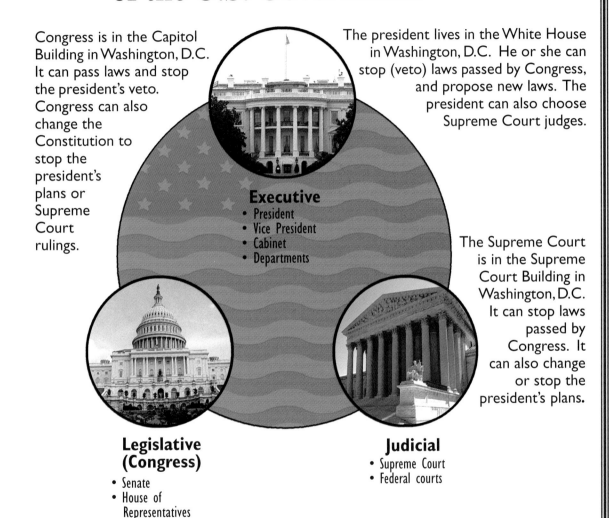

Congress is in the Capitol Building in Washington, D.C. It can pass laws and stop the president's veto. Congress can also change the Constitution to stop the president's plans or Supreme Court rulings.

The president lives in the White House in Washington, D.C. He or she can stop (veto) laws passed by Congress, and propose new laws. The president can also choose Supreme Court judges.

Executive
- President
- Vice President
- Cabinet
- Departments

The Supreme Court is in the Supreme Court Building in Washington, D.C. It can stop laws passed by Congress. It can also change or stop the president's plans.

Legislative (Congress)
- Senate
- House of Representatives

Judicial
- Supreme Court
- Federal courts

The U.S. Constitution formed three government branches. Each branch has power over the others. So no single group or person can control the country. The Constitution calls this "separation of powers."

A Politician to the End

*A*fter Van Buren left the White House, he still worked in **politics**. In 1844, he decided to run for president again.

Van Buren spoke against **annexing** Texas. He was still worried it would become a slave state. Some **Democrats** disagreed with him. They wanted to annex Texas and make the U.S. larger.

Van Buren's views made him unpopular. The Democrats did not **nominate** him for president. Instead, they nominated James K. Polk. Polk won the election.

Texas was annexed to the U.S. in 1845. This action split the Democratic party into two groups, the Hunkers and the Barnburners.

Van Buren led the Barnburners. The Barnburners wanted to stop slavery from spreading. They nominated Van Buren for president in 1848. But Van Buren's strong views had upset many Americans. He lost the election.

Van Buren spent the next several years traveling in Europe. He returned to Kinderhook in 1855. He worked on a book about his life in **politics**. It was called *Autobiography*. Van Buren died at Kinderhook on July 24, 1862.

Martin Van Buren served his country well. He worked his way from county **surrogate** to U.S. president. He led America through the Panic of 1837, troubles with Canada, and wars with Native Americans. His leadership strengthened America.

Van Buren retired to his mansion Lindenwald after the presidency.

Fast Facts

- Van Buren had the **nickname** Old Kinderhook. During the election of 1840, people shortened it to O.K. They started O.K. Clubs in support of Van Buren. Later, O.K. began to mean "all right."

- Van Buren threw away all of the red furniture in the White House. He changed everything to blue, creating the Blue Room.

- Because he was known for planning behind the scenes, Van Buren earned the nickname The Little Magician.

- Years after Van Buren's birth, the writer Washington Irving visited Kinderhook. He made it the setting of his famous story, "The Legend of Sleepy Hollow."

The Blue Room still exists in the White House today.

Glossary

advisor - a person who makes suggestions or gives advice.

annex - to add land to a nation.

apprentice - a person who learns a trade or craft from a skilled worker.

attorney general - the chief lawyer of a nation or state.

bar exam - the test that a person must pass in order to become a lawyer.

committee - a group of people chosen to do one special task.

compromise - settling an argument by having both sides give up some of what they want.

Congress - the lawmaking body of the U.S. It is made up of the Senate and the House of Representatives.

convention - a large meeting held for a special purpose.

debt - something owed to someone, usually money. A person who owes a debt is called a debtor.

declare - to make a formal, public announcement.

Democrat - a political party. When Van Buren was president, Democrats supported farmers and landowners.

depression - a period of economic trouble, when there is little buying and selling and many people are out of work.

Federalist - a political party active in the U.S. during the early 1800s. Federalists believed in strong national government.

Kitchen Cabinet - a group of politicians and friends who gave advice to President Jackson.

lawyer - a person who knows the laws and acts for another person in a court of law.

nickname - a name that in some way describes a person, that is used instead of his or her real name.

nominate - to name as a candidate for an office.

political machine - a group of party members, led by one boss, who have control of a city, county, or state.

politics - the process of making laws and running a government. A person who works in politics is a politician.

Republican - a political party. During Van Buren's time, Republicans favored a small federal government and state's rights. It became the Democratic party.

reservation - a piece of land set aside by the government for Native Americans.

secretary of state - a member of the president's cabinet who helps decide economic matters.

senator - a member of a governing or lawmaking assembly.

spoils system - a way of giving people jobs or taking them away because of political beliefs.

surrogate - a type of judge who settles disputes over estates and property rights.

transportation - the movement of something from one place to another.

treasury - a place where money is kept.

treaty - a formal agreement between two countries.

unite - to join together.

volunteer - to offer one's services.

War of 1812 - a war fought between 1812 and 1814 between the U.S. and Great Britain over shipping rights and the capture of U.S. soldiers.

Internet Sites

The Presidents of the United States of America
http://www.whitehouse.gov/WH/glimpse/presidents/html/presidents.html
This site is from the White House.

PBS American Presidents Series
http://www.americanpresident.org/KoTrain/Courses/MVB/MVB_In_Brief.htm
This site from PBS has links and information about Van Buren's life and elections.

The Martin Van Buren National Historic Site
http://www.nps.gov/mava/
Hosted by the National Park Service.

These sites are subject to change. Go to your favorite search engine and type in United States Presidents for more sites.

Index